SPOKANE
SKETCHBOOK

Drawings and architectural observations by
Roland Colliander, David Evans,
John Remington, Jim Waymire
Text by Thomas Stave

UNIVERSITY OF WASHINGTON PRESS · *Seattle and London*

Library of Congress Cataloging in Publication Data
Main entry under title:

Spokane sketchbook.

    1.   Architecture—Spokane.   2.   Spokane—Description—Views.
I. Colliander, Roland, 1939-   II. Stave, Thomas, 1947-
NA735.S64S64   720'9797'37   73-22207
ISBN 0-295-95326-8

To Spokane

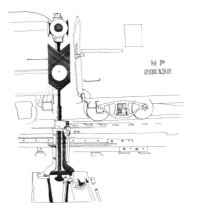

N P
201192

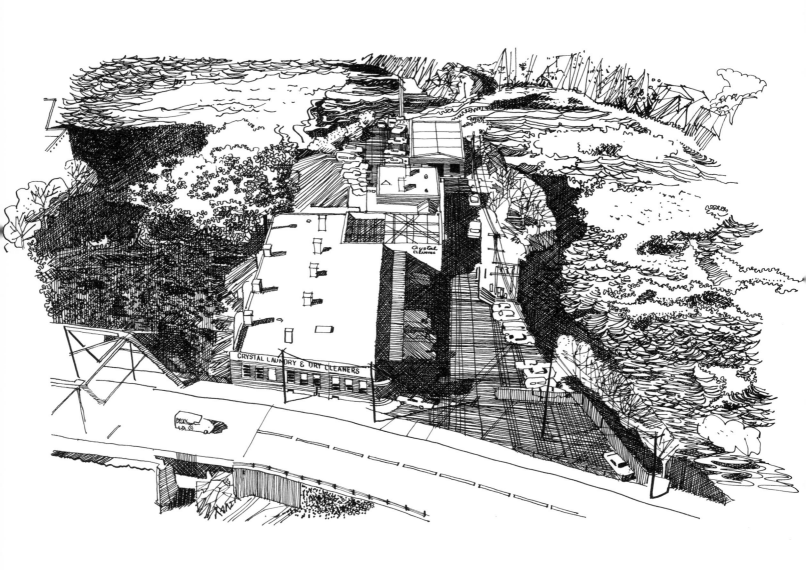

SPOKANE SKETCHBOOK

The first settlers of Spokane were fond of praising the natural delights of their new home. Their journals and letters are crowded with descriptions of the breath-taking waterfalls, plentiful fish and game, giant rock formations, acres of grasses and wildflowers. Since 1873, when James Nettle Glover gave the name Spokane Falls to the first permanent settlement, the city has been developing a new aspect, as appealing in many ways as its natural one. This new aspect, composed of the changes man has made in the landscape of Spokane, is the subject of this book. We look at the city through the eyes of architects, seeing its faults, but even more aware of its unique and admirable features that are largely taken for granted. We could not include everything we would have liked. There is enough material in the city for half a dozen such books.

Spokane's beauty consists of some very fine architecture and parks in a natural setting rivaled by few other cities. From near the edge of a mountainous pine forest the city looks south and west toward vast wheatlands. Its terrain is not gentle, but jagged and irregular, and its rocky bones pierce the surface prominently. Its gravel and clay are not kind to plants; only hardy ones grow here by choice: bunch grass, sunflowers, Ponderosa pine. Steep hills and palisades rise above the center of attention, the plunging Spokane River, which drops 150 feet over falls in the middle of town. It is a young landscape, calling to mind the forces of fire and ice that created it.

Spokane is a northern city, very nearly a Canadian one. Its northern latitude and its isolation from the moderating effects of warm ocean currents give it a dry climate characterized by a wide temperature range and precipitation that comes mainly in the form of snow. The people here live close to the seasons, which come and go with fanfare. Summers and winters must be reckoned with; spring arrives with a flourish, but is not official until the lilacs bloom, sometimes in fortunate concurrence with May's Lilac Festival.

The fact that Spokane is an inland city, isolated by great mountain ranges, may account for its rather home-grown character. Spokane's style reflects the qualities of its neighborhood: the independence of the wheat farmers; the enterprise of the miners; the sense of frontier fostered by the pine forests; the tenacity of the rock-clinging plants; the conservatism of isolation; and, occasionally, the flamboyance of its dashing, glittery, early days. There are some who think it is too slow-moving, but others feel grateful that Spokane does not suffer the ill effects of too much progress.

When Expo '74 was first proposed, it seemed to many to be a step out of character. Spokane was not considered to be "that kind of town." Perhaps that self-image persists. But the fact that the city decided to go ahead and produce a world's fair suggests that Spokane is beginning to look at itself with a more appreciative eye.

For a short but agonizing period of time in 1972, Spokane debated fiercely the fate of two of its oldest and handsomest buildings. The Great Northern Railway Station and Tower, built on Havermale Island in 1901, and the Union Pacific Railway Station, built opposite it across the river in 1915, were scheduled for demolition to make room for Expo '74. In the end the cold economic realities were louder than the voices of sentimental attachment, and the stations came down. The 160-foot Great Northern Tower, however, was left standing as a "reminder and tribute" to the sorts of things that plaque-makers will surely think up. And there are dozens of historical people and events for whom a plaque near the tower would be appropriate. But at that important place three things seem particularly worth remembering: the first settlement in Spokane, one block away; the Spokane River, which attracted the Indians here with its fish and the white men with its source of cheap power; and the railroads, which, aside from linking Spokane with Chicago and the West Coast, created a web of economic and social relationships that collectively constitute the "Inland Empire." Far from being a purely imaginary realm, the Inland Empire is Spokane's reason for existence. The city owed its early growth to its role as transporter and supplier for the farmers, miners, and lumbermen between the Rockies and the Cascades, and it still depends primarily upon its ability to serve the same region with goods, transportation, power, health services, entertainment, and government functions.

The Union Pacific Station *(below)* once stood at the corner of Trent and Stevens, the elegant hub of an active passenger rail service. Directly across the river was the Great Northern Station and Tower, designed by the architects Dawson and Granger.

"Old 3206" served Union Pacific for fifty years. Donated by the railroad to the city, it sits out its retirement in High Bridge Park.

Seventy miles southeast of Spokane, on the South Fork of the Coeur d'Alene River in the heart of Idaho's mountainous silver-, lead-, and zinc-mining district, is the town of Wallace. For years this railway station has served the town and mines that gave it its first name, Placer City.

U.S. 410 makes a T in Waitsburg, forcing the motorist to slow down and catch more than just a glimpse of this simple, uncluttered little town. Waitsburg is one of the state's oldest towns and one of only two cities in the United States still operating under its territorial charter.

The time is past when simple wooden railway stations were the center of activity for most towns in the Northwest. Through good fortune and community concern, this one has survived unblemished by deterioration or remodeling when most of its kind have disappeared. The station was built sometime after 1882 when the Union Pacific Railway came to the city of Dayton in the grain, orchard, and pea-growing region of southeastern Washington.

The Palouse Country's uniquely fertile soil is a by-product of the volcanic eruptions that raised the Cascade Mountains millions of years ago. The fine dust spewed by Mounts Rainier, Adams, St. Helens, and Hood was deposited in deep layers over this region, which spreads southward from Spokane to the Snake River, and there is now no finer wheat country in the world. But hard times come even to tillers of the world's richest wheatland. As a result the farms have become bigger and fewer, as is witnessed by abandoned schools and farmhouses such as these.

Round barn near Steptoe

These hulking giants are as much a part of the wheat country landscape as the gentle hills that surround them and the small towns that huddle at their feet. There is a utilitarian kind of beauty in these elevators because they do so well what they were built to do.

Combines, too, have long been part of the Palouse scene. The heavy wooden horse- or mule-drawn proto-type only vaguely resembled today's version with its air-conditioned cab and self-leveling device that auto-matically takes account of the Palouse's uneven terrain.

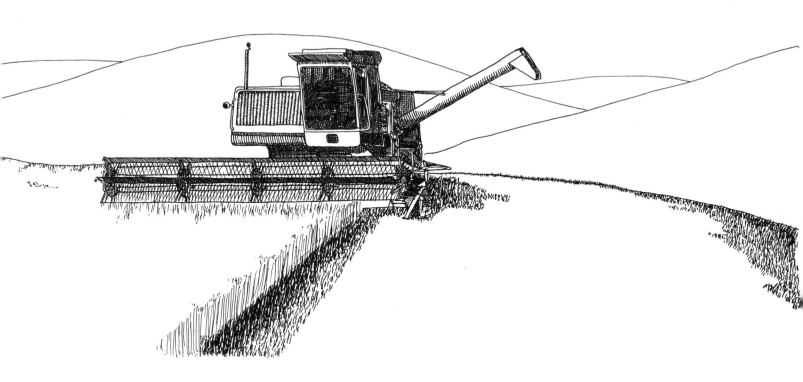

Palouse sunset

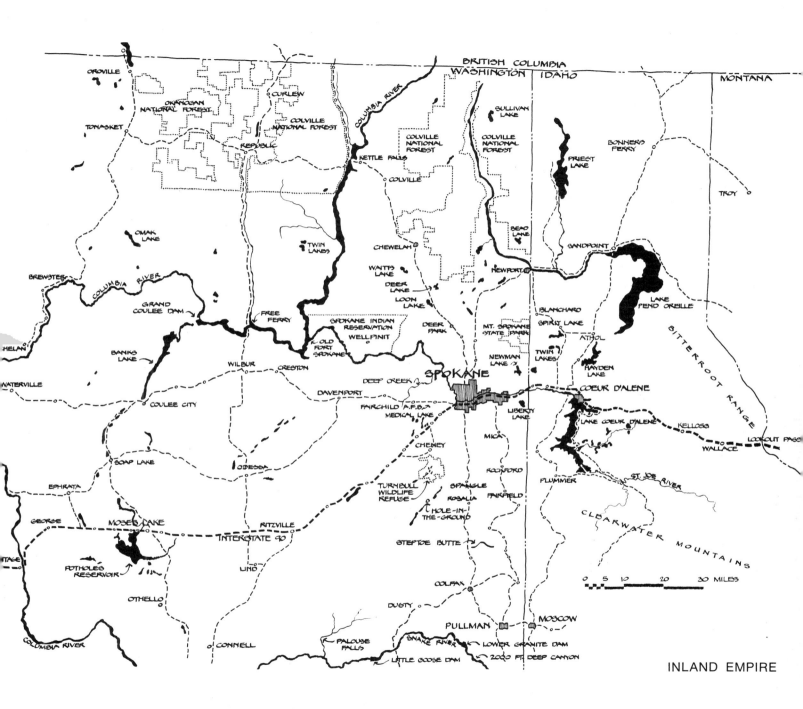

INLAND EMPIRE

The greatest surface lava flow in the history of the world created these orderly formations of basalt columns. Between ten and fifteen million years ago molten rock poured through great cracks miles long into what is now eastern Washington and Oregon, covering the 200,000-square-mile area to a depth of half a mile. In many places the lava cracked as it cooled, producing regularly shaped columns like these seen from State Highway 2 near the Spokane International Airport.

Another later flow left the Bowl and Pitcher formation in Riverside State Park on the city's west side. They are fine specimens of ''pillow basalt,'' which occurs when hot lava spills into water.

When an Ice Age glacier forced the Spokane River to leave its channel downriver from Spokane, it cut a deep canyon into its high basalt bank. Though the river no longer follows this course, Deep Creek Canyon is now the route by which a small stream flows through some of the area's most fantastic scenery to find the Spokane River. And during spring runoff its frightening torrents are enough to make believers out of any who doubt that those massive rock figures were carved by mere water.

DEEP CREEK CANYON
← 15 MILES →

SPOKANE RIVER

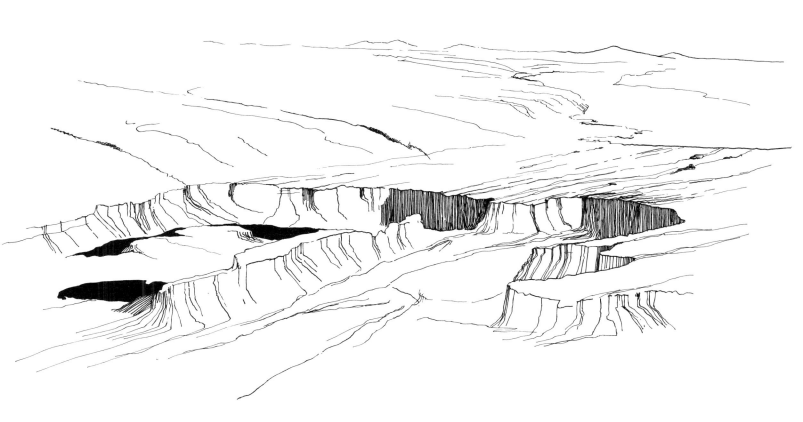

Another glacier of that period dammed the Pend Oreille River in northern Idaho, creating a lake that backed up 250 miles, filling mountain valleys to a depth of 2,500 feet. After long centuries the dam failed because a series of warm summers had weakened the ice so that it could no longer withstand the pressure that had built up behind it. When it collapsed, a terrific flood coursed through the Spokane Valley and ravaged eastern Washington with hundreds of cubic miles of water. After only a week the lake's waters were spent and the Spokane Flood was over, a flood perhaps unique in the history of the world in its magnitude and destructive power. Dry Falls, one hundred miles to the west of Spokane, may have been one of its results.

Large basalt "haystacks," like these in front of St. Luke's Hospital, are actually some of the larger boulders that owe their unusual locations to glacial movers. The huge sheets of ice that four times advanced as far as Spokane, but no farther, left these enormous rocks flung about like toys scattered by a child. Many Spokane designers, greatly to their credit, have treated the haystacks not as inconveniences but rather as assets, designing buildings in sympathy with them.

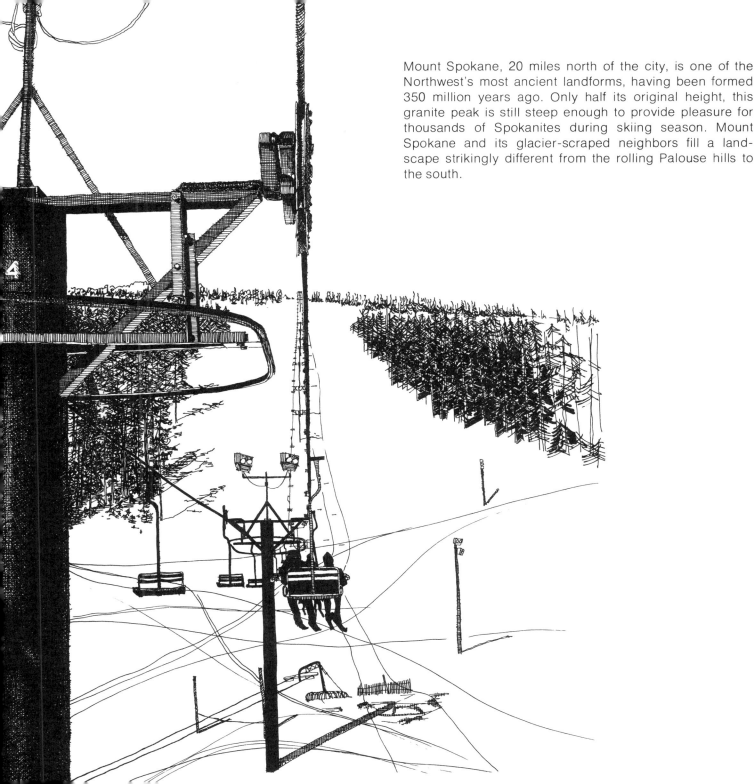

Mount Spokane, 20 miles north of the city, is one of the Northwest's most ancient landforms, having been formed 350 million years ago. Only half its original height, this granite peak is still steep enough to provide pleasure for thousands of Spokanites during skiing season. Mount Spokane and its glacier-scraped neighbors fill a landscape strikingly different from the rolling Palouse hills to the south.

If Spokane seems deserted for the ski slopes in the winter, its abandonment on summer weekends is almost complete. The warm weather attraction is the score of nearby glacially carved lakes. More than most cities, Spokane is oriented to the out-of-doors, perhaps because it is so easily available.

In 1909 August Paulsen, made wealthy by his Idaho silver mines, built the Paulsen Professional Building on Riverside Avenue. He directed architects John K. Dow and C. Z. Hubbell to design the "best eleven-story office building money could build." It was billed as Spokane's first skyscraper. Twenty years later Paulsen topped it by building next door. The sixteen-story Paulsen Medical and Dental Building, designed by G. A. Pehrson, contains a small hospital and medical library. The large penthouse was for many years the luxury home of Mrs. August Paulsen.

One thing that can give visual unity to a city is color, and a close look will show that in Spokane the reds have predominated. While no one expects every new building to follow closely that precedent, it is worth noting when a design does pay special attention to the continuity of the color scheme, as does the Pacific National Bank of Washington at Riverside and Post. Behind the bank designed by the firm of Trogdon–Smith–Grossman is a quiet little plaza built around a Harold Balazs welded copper sculpture.

The Farm Credit Banks Building on First and Wall is constructed of dark tinted glass and concrete faced with white granite. The second, third, and fourth floors, each overhanging the one below it, house three farm credit banks. The lobby, which extends the full height of the building, is shared by all three. Two concrete bridges crossing sunken gardens below street level provide entrances to the building. This structure, bold and refined, was designed by Walker, McGough, Foltz and Lyerla.

This pedestrian plaza off Howard and Riverside was built to complement the Parkade parking garage in 1967. Immediately it became the unofficial center of activity for downtown Spokane.

Architect Warren Heylman designed the structure with people more in mind than cars. The street level is given to small shops, and the entrance and exit ramps are created so as not to interfere with the pedestrian traffic. But the real people place is outside the shops, beneath the Parkade's spiral ramp and flared concrete columns, around the spilling fountain on the patterned brick floor of the plaza.

Here on sunny afternoons the whole mosaic of Spokane life appears: all ages, all types, all reasons. There is no more perfectly suitable place in town to meet for lunch, stage a rock concert, talk over business, preach the end of the world, garner votes, bum a dime, or simply watch people.

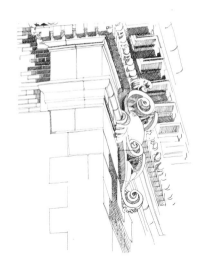

The ornate terra-cotta facing and cornice work of the School District Building *(right)* testify to the skill of some anonymous craftsmen who pursued their trade around Spokane at the turn of the century. Built in 1906 as the Washington Water Power Company's original home office building, it now provides administrative offices for Spokane School District 81. Kirtland Cutter and Karl G. Malmgren designed this building, which overlooks the falls at Lincoln and Trent. Another Cutter-Malmgren project stands a block away, the Washington Water Power Substation *(left),* whose utilitarian purpose is well expressed in the brick design. The sketch omits a neon sign that tops the building.

Detail of the Sherwood Building, another Cutter design

For many years the sides of Spokane's brick buildings of-
fered the most convenient advertising space in town, as
well as a livelihood for some talented but now forgotten
painters. Examples of their work still abound in Spokane
because of the numerous suitable buildings that still exist.
In fact, if one were to create a composite structure in-
cluding Spokane's most typical architectural features, it
would probably be a 1910 six-story brick. Although Spokane's architectural genius has been chiefly expressed in
other forms, this sort of building is a key to the character
of the city.

Many city dwellers miss some of the fine things of the city because they keep their gazes below the level of canopies, marquees, and neon signs. On Wall Street above Sartori Jewelers, looking out over the concrete and glass store fronts, is a mostly unnoticed façade. This building rises six stories high, yet is only sixteen feet wide. There is a reason for its unusually narrow face. Years ago the site was donated for an alleyway. Buildings eventually rose on either side, but the alley never materialized. In 1907 the owners of the abutting Hyde Building built in the space a structure to contain their lavatories. The designer, a free spirit, faced those lavatories with some of the most ornate terra cotta and brick in the city.

Second City is a delightful exception to the rule that down-town Spokane's second stories are filled with dust and memories. This meandering assemblage of shops and stalls has revitalized the quarters above First and Howard that the University Club abandoned years ago. Second City is not just Spokane's chic downtown shop district, nor is it merely an imitation of other West Coast shop complexes designed to be fashionably hidden in old alleys and stairwells. While certainly chic and out-of-the-way, these shops would be remarkable in any location for more important reasons.

They are run by a talented community of shopkeeper-artists who express in their shops and wares strong personal principles of beauty, taste, and craftsmanship. One senses here that the chance to live by their hands and skills and to create their pieces in a stimulating, encouraging environment means more than income—indeed, some can scarcely pay the rent. But they have made the happy discovery that several small concerns under a single roof prosper better than as many scattered ventures. Spokane is the biggest beneficiary of Second City's success. In these weavers, painters, and carvers; these workers of clay, leather, and metal; Spokane has gained a new standard of individual craftsmanship and enterprise.

Many older Spokane buildings are being renovated to serve newer uses and tastes. In refurbishing the Sons of Norway Hall on Riverside Avenue, the architectural firm of Walker, McGough, Foltz and Lyerla saved its fine old façade.

The Post Office Building at Lincoln and Riverside was considered by some to be the most beautiful building in the city when it was built in 1909. Like most other federal buildings of its time, the Post Office (and then Federal Courthouse) was erected along classical lines of Bedford limestone. Although the courtrooms have since moved and the building is too small for the current needs of the Postal Service, it remains an enduring and honored part of Spokane.

Riverside Avenue looking east from the Review
Building

Riverside Avenue, looking past the Great Western Clock and Review Building, across Monroe Street toward Our Lady of Lourdes Cathedral

When the Review Building was built in 1891 to house the newspaper (now the *Spokesman-Review)*, it was the most conspicuous building in town. Its seven stories, peaked roof, and tower were of French Renaissance design, expressed in red brick and gray Montana granite. The front of the building was curved to conform to the flow of Riverside Avenue. Behind the curved glass windows the interior was made lavish with white, yellow, and red marble; art glass; cherry wood; imported English tile; and bronze hardwood.

At its location on Riverside and Monroe, the Review Building serves to divide the "two Riverside Avenues." It is actually the western anchor of that street's business district, which marches off to the east. But the elegant and imposing red tower is equally appropriate to Riverside's more sedate and graceful neighborhood across Monroe. There the Spokane Club, Our Lady of Lourdes Catholic Cathedral, and the Chancery Building watch one another across the street's tree-lined dividing park. Farther along are the Chamber of Commerce, Elk's Club, Masonic Temple, and Red Cross Chapter Building.

Our Lady of Lourdes Catholic Cathedral, the Cathedral Church for the Diocese of Spokane, was built in 1908. It was built in Italian Romanesque design of granite and red brick. Seen from a suitable vantage point, its twin towers offer a fine balance to the spires of the Courthouse across the river.

Architect J. K. Dow drew the original design for the Masonic Temple in 1903, calling for a pure Roman style of the Imperial period. When in 1925 the firm of Rigg and Vantyne doubled the building's capacity, the effect was to lengthen the two-storied Corinthian loggias without altering the basic design. The materials are enameled ivory terra cotta and light buff brick. Two structures of equal interest flank the building: on its right the Chamber of Commerce and on its left the Elk's Club.

Overlooking the Spokane River at Riverside and Monroe is the city's oldest club. Founded in 1890, the Spokane Club moved in 1910 to its present building, a Kirtland Cutter design.

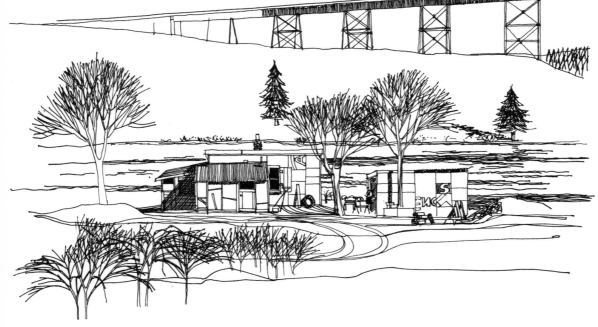

A minute's walk down the hill from West Riverside's affluent clubs and apartments is the neighborhood known as Peaceful Valley. Cut off from the mainstream of Spokane life by its isolated situation at the foot of the riverbank, it has been a depressed area since the days when it was less euphemistically called Poverty Flats. Still, its character is amiable, and many old residents prefer it.

"There they lost a pack horse, and while old man Kellogg went in search of it, up Elk gulch, Phil started the hunt up Milo gulch. At the head of the creek he found some galena float. Though it was dreadful hard work to get through the brush and fallen timber, he climbed up the hill about 500 feet, and there he stumbled upon the great Bunker Hill ledge, sticking right up out of the ground. There was nothing in sight but glittering galena, and O'Rourke knew he had found the greatest thing ever discovered in the northwest'' (''Dutch Jake'' Goetz's account of the discovery of the Bunker Hill-Sullivan Mine, 1885).

It was lead, not gold, in Idaho's Coeur d'Alene Mountains that produced Spokane's great wealth in the late 1800s. But it was reports of placer gold circulated widely by the Northern Pacific Railway that brought in trainloads of bright-eyed miners from the east to be outfitted in Spokane and, most likely, to be out of luck in the mines. Many mines produced—and still do —and some few men became wealthy.

The large number of beautiful old mansions in Spokane, like this one built for James Glover, is due to the coincidence of three events: the Coeur d'Alene mine discoveries that created dozens of instant millionaires, the great fire of 1889, and the arrival from the East of a young architectural genius named Kirtland Kelsey Cutter.

Daniel Chase Corbin was not a miner. But when he arrived in the Coeur d'Alenes in 1886 he recognized the need for transporting all that metal, so he built the region's first railroad and made his fortune. He built his brick Georgian house with porches on three sides against a rock cliff on Seventh Avenue. Corbin's house has become the Park Department's Art Center, and his front yard is now Pioneer Park.

After the fire of 1889, Spokane's young capitalists were eager to rebuild in a way that would show off their raw wealth to the world, and Cutter had the sophistication and imagination to do it for them. Perhaps the least restrained of the newly prosperous miners was Patrick Clark, whose residence at West 2208 Second Avenue enjoyed every luxury that was conceivable in 1898. Clark sent Cutter to Europe to buy furnishings and material for his Moorish mansion. He brought back sandstone from Italy, European carved wood, Turkish rugs, Louis XIV furniture, an English grandfather clock, and a French artist to paint cherubs on the ceilings. The house is now a catering establishment, the Francis Lester Inn. Cutter himself was not embarrassed by his own new-found prosperity. His residence was a Swiss-style chalet which has since been torn down to make room for an apartment building.

This pillar (*below*), one of two that mark the entrance to Rockwood Boulevard at Eleventh Avenue, was erected in 1905 when the neighborhood was new. In the 1920s Rockwood Addition was Spokane's most elite district. A meandering drive up Rockwood Boulevard is still rewarded with glimpses of old palatial homes.

Around the turn of the century, Spokane's wealthy built their homes in one of two neighborhoods. Some, like Corbin and Cutter, chose the area around Seventh Avenue, known as "the Hill." Others, such as Patrick Clark and Amasa B. Campbell, settled near West First Avenue in the district called "Browne's Addition." The rivalry between the two was fierce. Campbell's house *(right)* was designed by Cutter with the stucco and timbers of the Elizabethan style. It is now owned by the Cowles Museum of the Eastern Washington Historical Society, which offers frequent tours of the well-restored house.

Browne's Addition on the left and the South Hill on the right greet the visitor who enters Spokane from the west. The western approach is surely the most dramatic, taking a long slow descent until, just before Hangman Creek Bridge, the entire city is suddenly unveiled. Ben Garnett, former city bridge engineer, designed the concrete span, one of the most magnificent in a city of bridges. It is a sobering thought that, but for some well-directed public outrage, an earth fill would have occupied its place.

"It is a universally recognized fact that an essential feature of a city is the provision for ample open spaces for recreation and the promotion of public health.

"The Spokane Park System was undertaken . . . with the thought in the minds of its sponsors of securing, while they could, such areas as would not only be adequate for the city of present time, but for the century to come" (Aubrey L. White, first Spokane Park Board President, 1927).

Manito Park's loop drive crosses itself at the basalt bridge, which is a true arch, built without the aid of mortar.

Among Spokane's parks, Manito's place of honor is so well established that it is known among park people simple as "The Park." With its playfields, duckpond, natural areas, and formal and informal gardens, it is really many parks, which are multiplied wonderfully with every change in the season.

Among the finest of their kind in the country are the formal Duncan Gardens, named after John W. Duncan, a former superintendent of parks. The Italian fountain, a memorial to Louis Davenport, was designed by H. C. Whitehouse.

Ponderosa pines, along with the great basalt haystacks, are first citizens of Spokane. These friendly giants, more than any other features of the landscape, are natural emblems of the city. They are suited by their long roots to the dry regions east of the Cascades, and they often reach 150 feet by their two-hundredth birthdays. But they have no similar protection against the smoke and fumes to which they are so pitifully vulnerable. You can tell the Ponderosa pine by its noble height and by the foot-long needles, growing in bundles, that are incomparable against a blue summer sky.

Just off Ben Garnett Way at South Thirteenth, in tiny Cliff Park, is Review Rock, Spokane's highest point. From this sudden rocky knoll with its cliff-like sides can be seen the entire north side of the city and, farther off, Mount Spokane and the more distant Canadian peaks. To the east, beyond St. John's Cathedral, the Spokane River Valley spreads out toward Idaho. Geologists speculate that Cliff Park was formed by an eddy of the great Spokane Flood a million years ago.

Finch Arboretum: there is no finer place in Spokane than this mile-long strip of lawns and trees along Garden Springs Creek, and no better time to spend an afternoon there than when the lilacs, hawthorn, azaleas, rhododendron, cherry, plum, and crabapple are blooming.

The Spokane Indians, after whom the city was named, still honor Spokane with occasional visits, as in this encampment at Franklin Park.

The Episcopal Cathedral of St. John the Evangelist stands sentinel-like on the crest of the South Hill. Constructed between 1925 and 1955, it was built to succeed All Saints Cathedral, which served the Spokane Episcopal Missionary District from 1893 to 1929. Harold C. Whitehouse of the firm Whitehouse and Price designed the classical English Gothic cathedral.

St. John's interior walls are of Idaho sandstone, and the exterior stones were carved from full-scale drawings at the sandstone quarries in Tacoma. The rose window above the west entrance is the work of Charles J. Connick. Its delicate pattern disguises the fact that its 124 pieces weigh over thirteen tons. The cathedral is 258 feet long and 125 feet wide at the transepts, and its tower reaches a height of 168 feet above the floor of the nave. But such dimensions are meaningless when one stands on the stone floor of the crossing, gazing up at the carved stone and the brilliant rose window. That is an experience produced nowhere else in Spokane.

Gonzaga University on East Boone Avenue is one of four four-year colleges in the Spokane area, the others being Whitworth College, Fort George Wright College of the Holy Names, and Eastern Washington State College. Gonzaga's Administration Building *(below and below, right)* was begun in 1897, ten years after Father Joseph Cataldo founded the college. In 1903, already one of the largest Jesuit colleges in the country, Gonzaga expanded the four-story brick building with its solid granite foundation to make room for a growing student body. The firm of Preusse and Zittel were architects for both phases of construction.

The John F. Kennedy Memorial Pavilion and Pool *(above),* designed by the Spokane firm of McClure and Adkison, was built in 1965.

St. Aloysius Catholic Church at Boone and Astor is part of the Gonzaga University campus. Dedicated in 1911, it was built in an adapted Romanesque design of brick which is of the same color and material as the other college buildings.

The First Presbyterian Church at Fourth and Cedar was built in 1910. Its modified Gothic design was conceived by an out-of-town architect, but altered to suit local conditions by Spokane architect L. L. Rand.

The Unitarian Church of Spokane is effectively screened from busy Eighth Avenue by its landscaping and its form, which seem to blend together. The church, a McClure-Adkison design, is in good company, with the IBM Building, Comstock Arms, and the Cutter-designed Glover House for neighbors.

Temple Beth Shalom at East 1322 Thirtieth houses the union of two Jewish congregations, Congregation Keneseth Israel and Temple Emanu-El. Freeway construction condemned the old home, and in 1969 the present building, a Walker, McGough, Foltz and Lyerla design, was dedicated.

From 1908 to 1968 thousands were entertained on the carrousel at Natatorium Park. Nat Park's gayway, big band dances, and Fourth of July fireworks over the river have since given way to a trailer park, but the carrousel will see new life. After five years in storage, the world's last hand-carved, self-enclosed carrousel is being restored to take its place on the site of Expo '74. It was designed and built in Rhode Island by a German wood carver, C. H. Looff, who gave it four Chinese dragons, a giraffe, a tiger, and fifty-four horses, all different. The horses are so realistically fashioned that you can tell the age of each by its teeth. When Looff's carrousel was completed, he packed it up and sent it to Spokane as a wedding present for his daughter.

The Spokane County Courthouse, commanding the river's north bank, is an example of pure French Renaissance design. The magnificent structure resembles two chateaux built in France in the early sixteenth century. It was built in 1894 when a courthouse design contest was won by a young architect named Willis A. Ritchie. His towers and turrets are impressive from a distance, and are best appreciated from the immediate south bank, but a closer viewing will reveal a wealth of detailed iron and brickwork whose craftsmanship could not be duplicated today at any cost. Recent removal of the elevated railroad tracks along Trent Street has made the courthouse again visible from downtown, and perhaps future sympathetic development of the riverfront land near Monroe Street will create a more proper setting for this sculpturesque building.

In 1917 Louis Davenport opened the hotel that brought Spokane its reputation as "the city built around a hotel." That perhaps overstates the case, but this internationally known building has certainly signified Spokane for decades to thousands of visitors. Davenport spared nothing to build what he considered the finest hotel in America. The first two floors are of stone, and the remainder of brick trimmed with terra cotta, all in a handsome Florentine design. The building's real charm, however, is the interior. The lobby, while certainly luxurious, still manages to be both intimate and domestic. The ballroom and banquet rooms are beautifully created in Spanish, Elizabethan, and Italian Renaissance styles. In the opinion of some, however, the Davenport is a grand old lady who has outlived her day, old-world elegance trying to survive in an age of motels. In any case, she is for now a well-loved landmark and a testimony to Davenport's entrepreneurial imagination and Kirtland Cutter's architectural genius.

In the ashes of the 1889 fire, which demolished thirty-two city blocks, Louis M. Davenport opened a small restaurant in a tent. From this "waffle foundry," for which he was cashier, cook, waiter, and dishwasher, grew the establishment which in 1908 was acclaimed as "the best, the most unique and nearly perfect restaurant in America—and perhaps the world." The Matador Restaurant and the Davenport Hotel are linked on the inside by a passageway and on the outside by the horizontal lines of Kirtland Cutter's design.

The Washington Water Power Building, which houses the utility's offices and service facilities, is located at East 1411 Mission on the north bank of the river. The structure was designed by Ken Brooks and Bruce Walker, with landscape design by Lawrence Halprin. The building design, landscape design, and site planning are excellent. Considering the nature of the structure and business, however, the necessity and tastefulness of the sign (not shown in the drawing) are questionable.

After having borne a century of civilization, the Spokane River and its banks still support populations of wild plants and animals within the city. The great migratory flocks of ducks and geese stop over here to feed in the fall and spring. Colonies of marmots inhabit the banks on and near Havermale Island, and porcupines have been sighted under the Monroe Street Bridge. Still here in abundance are the plants the Indians used for food, described by James Glover in 1873.

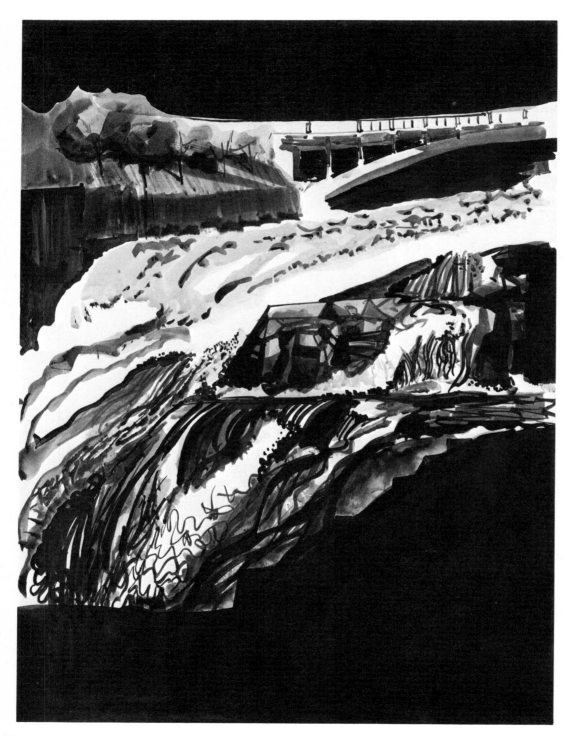

Spokane Falls

For several weeks in the spring of 1973, large crowds of people gathered on the Post Street Bridge. Most were watching the demolition of the Great Northern Railroad trestle, which for many years bore trains to and from the Havermale Island depot. But some had come to catch their first unobstructed glimpse of the upper Spokane Falls spilling around tiny Cannon Island. Early in its development Spokane had given up its view of the river for the privilege of running railroads through the center of town. Besides keeping the river a secret, however, the railroads had another more beneficial effect. In combination with the natural terrain, they effectively contained the sprawl of the downtown area—an uncontested blessing.

The Monroe Street Bridge, favorably positioned to show off its massive piers and arches and its well-detailed towers and balustrade, was built in 1912 under the direction of engineer J. C. Ralston and architect Kirtland Cutter to replace previous wood and steel spans. Viewed from the west, the bridge's concrete arches frame the Spokane River's lower falls; viewed from the east, they are a gateway for the Downriver Gorge. And the bridge itself is possibly the best vantage point for either sight.

Lying almost directly beneath the bridge, the Monroe Street Generating Plant might easily go unnoticed if it did not sit so near the falls. The plant's historical importance and durability have earned it the right to retain its privileged location. It went into operation in 1890 as the Washington Water Power Company's first hydroelectric generating plant and one of the earliest of its kind in the world. Washington Water Power had been formed when local stockholders broke off from an East Coast company whose members claimed there was no future in water power. The "smokestacks" are really surge tanks designed to contain excess water from the penstocks. They were removed when the building was modified in 1973.

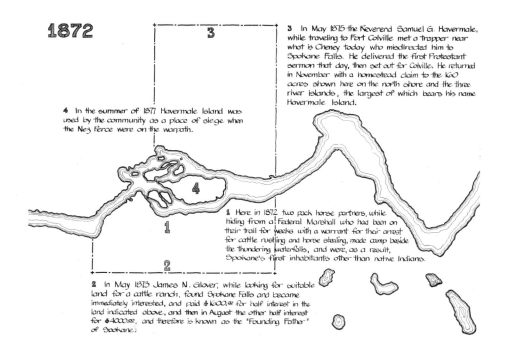

1872

3 In May 1875 the Reverend Samuel G. Havermale, while traveling to Fort Colville met a trapper near what is Cheney today who misdirected him to Spokane Falls. He delivered the first Protestant sermon that day, then set out for Colville. He returned in November with a homestead claim to the 160 acres shown here on the north shore and the three river islands, the largest of which bears his name Havermale Island.

4 In the summer of 1877 Havermale Island was used by the community as a place of siege when the Nez Perce were on the warpath.

1 Here in 1872 two pack horse partners, while hiding from a Federal Marshall who had been on their trail for weeks with a warrant for their arrest for cattle rustling and horse stealing, made camp beside the thundering waterfalls, and were, as a result, Spokane's first inhabitants other than native Indians.

2 In May 1873 James N. Glover, while looking for suitable land for a cattle ranch, found Spokane Falls and became immediately interested, and paid $1600.00 for half interest in the land indicated above, and then in August the other half interest for $4000.00, and therefore is known as the "Founding Father" of Spokane.

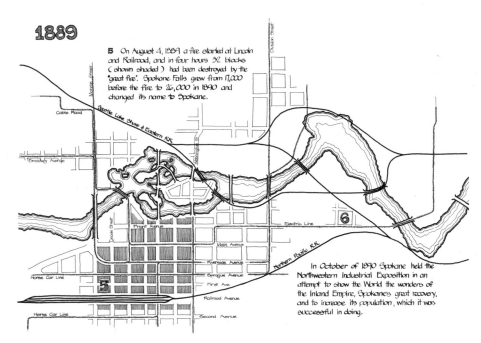

1889

5 On August 4, 1889 a fire started at Lincoln and Railroad, and in four hours 32 blocks (shown shaded) had been destroyed by the "great fire". Spokane Falls grew from 17,000 before the fire to 26,000 in 1890 and changed its name to Spokane.

In October of 1890 Spokane held the Northwestern Industrial Exposition in an attempt to show the World the wonders of the Inland Empire, Spokane's great recovery, and to increase its population, which it was successful in doing.

1971

By mid century Spokane Falls had become hidden under and behind railroad and vehicle bridges, and, deteriorated industrial and warehouse structures. It was virtually impossible to see the Falls. In the late 1960's the Riverfront Development Plan called for the return of the Spokane River to an improved condition with parks, walks and open space accessible to people again.

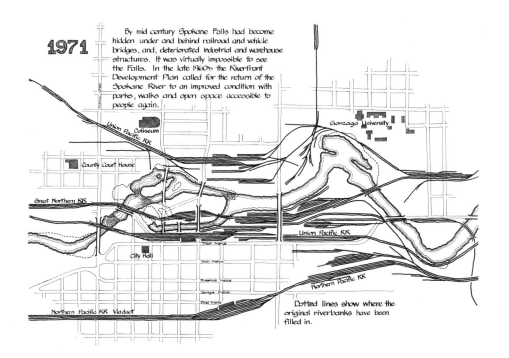

Dotted lines show where the original riverbanks have been filled in.

1975

Wall Street from Foot to Trent will be permanently vacated, as will Howard Street, and the Howard Street Bridges will be removed to clear the island of surface traffic, to open the area for pedestrian use.

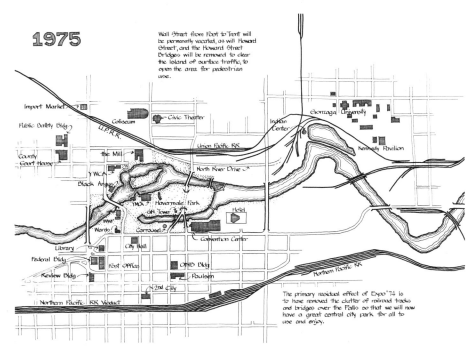

The primary residual effect of Expo '74 is to have removed the clutter of railroad tracks and bridges over the Falls so that we will now have a great central city park for all to use and enjoy.

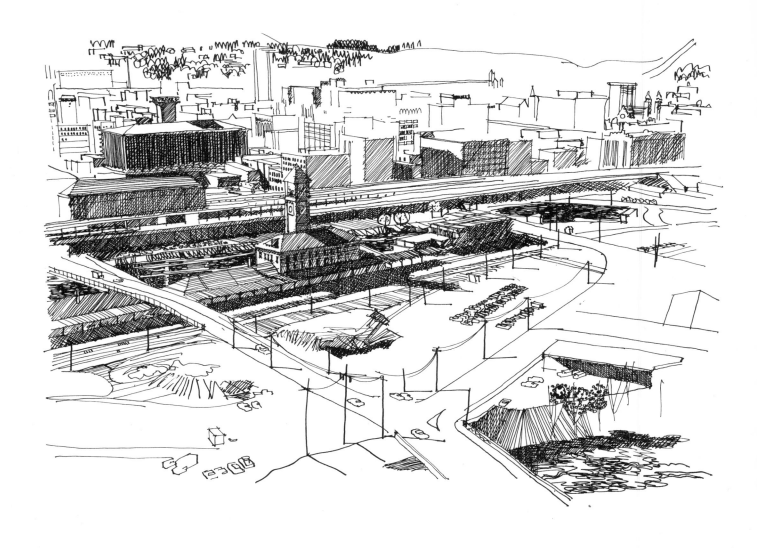

Strictly speaking, Havermale has not been an island since a landfill connected its west end with the south bank. Large penstocks carry water under this artificial isthmus to generator buildings downstream. When Havermale becomes a park it should regain the character if not the reality of an island. This sketch, looking south over Havermale Island to Trent Street, was made before Expo '74. None of these structures north of Trent exists any longer except the old Great Northern Tower.

The tower kept watch over the hectic demolition on Havermale during the year that everything came down, and in the end it was the only survivor.

Original conceptual design studies for the Spokane World
Exposition from the office of Thomas R. Adkison, Expo '74
Executive Site Architect

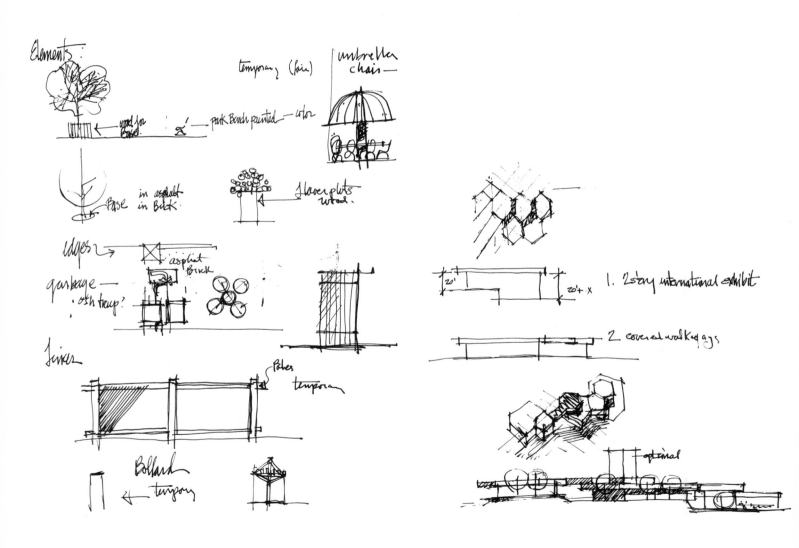

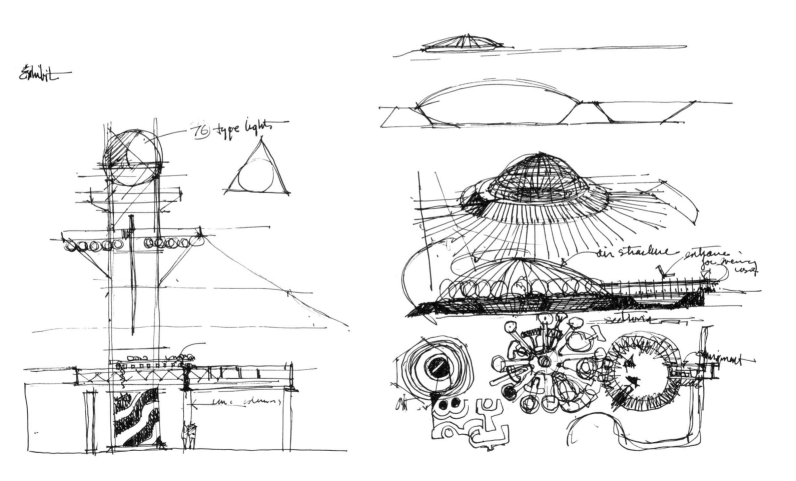

Exhibit

76 type lights

air structure

entrance

section

equipment

conc columns

91

South Channel portion of Expo '74 site, drawing from the office of Thomas R. Adkison, Expo '74 Executive Site Architect

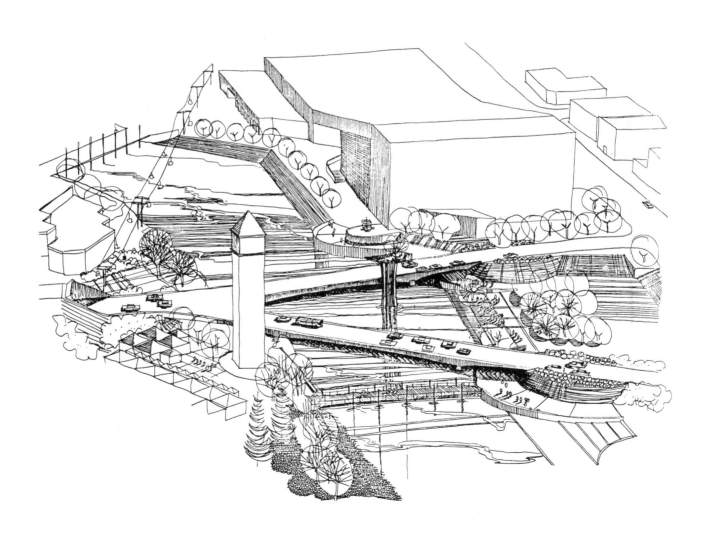

SPOKANE CITY LOOP DRIVE
approximately 30 miles or 3 hours

① Dramatic view of Spokane from the freeway entering from the west

② J. A. Finch Arboretum

③ Sunset Highway Bridge, Freeway Bridge, and Railroad Bridge over the canyon created by Latah Creek below

④ Cliff Drive with panorama of the city below and fine old mansions lining the cliff

⑤ Cliff Park – walk to the top for a wide view of the City. Highest elevation in this area of the City. Also of geological interest.

⑥ Manito Pond in Manito Park – see ducks etc., skating in the Winter

⑦ Manito Park – City's best, see the Rose Hill, Duncan Gardens and greenhouse

⑧ Japanese Garden – gift of Spokane's sister City: Nishinomiya, Japan

⑨ Cannon Hill Park – a fine residential small park with a pond, bridges and old stone park buildings

⑩ 21st Avenue – fine residential boulevard street

⑪ High Drive with fantastic view of Latah Creek below. Stop and walk along edge or stop in park across the street.

⑫ Comstock Park with swimming pool

⑬ High Drive Parkway with view of hills south and lined with some fine homes

⑭ Temple Beth Shalom – Contemporary Synagogue architecture

⑮ Rockwood Boulevard, lined by some of the City's finest early 20th century residences as well as new on the easterly extension of the street

⑯ Cathedral of St. John the Evangelist (Episcopal) – excellent Gothic architecture and beautiful stained glass windows.

⑰ St. Luke's Hospital – handsome contemporary concrete architecture

⑱ Central Business District

⑲ Expo '74 and future Central Park

⑳ Civic Theater

㉑ Coliseum

㉒ Audubon Park

㉓ Downriver Park and Riverside Municipal Golf Course

㉔ Entrance to A. L. White Parkway which leads down the river into Riverside State Park with miles of scenic and geological attractions

㉕ Spokane Falls Community College

㉖ Fort Wright College of the Holy Names – Site of early Army Base

㉗ Shrine Hospital & wide views of the Spokane River below

㉘ County Courthouse and Public Safety Building – high Architectural interest

㉙ Maple Street Bridge

㉚ Spokane Falls – Spectacular!

㉛ Cheney Cowles Museum and Grace Campbell Museum, conducted by the Eastern Washington State Historical Society — Collections of Indian arts, pioneer relics, and regional geology, and contemporary arts

㉜ Coeur d'Alene Park – City's oldest

㉝ High Bridge Park – old locomotive

㉞ Indian Canyon Golf Course

㉟ Palisades Park

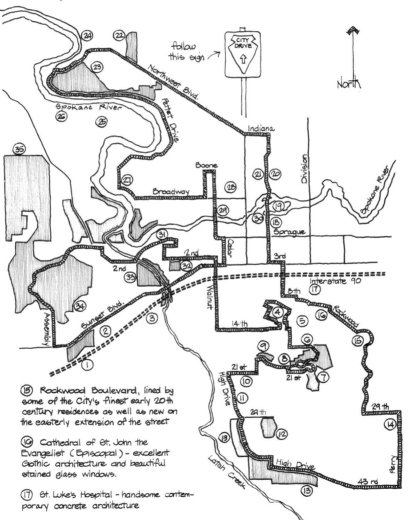

follow this sign →

North

93